ALL AROUND THE WORLD
LITHUANIA

by Kristine Spanier, MLIS

Ideas for Parents and Teachers

Pogo Books let children practice reading informational text while introducing them to nonfiction features such as headings, labels, sidebars, maps, and diagrams, as well as a table of contents, glossary, and index.

Carefully leveled text with a strong photo match offers early fluent readers the support they need to succeed.

Before Reading

- "Walk" through the book and point out the various nonfiction features. Ask the student what purpose each feature serves.
- Look at the glossary together. Read and discuss the words.

Read the Book

- Have the child read the book independently.
- Invite him or her to list questions that arise from reading.

After Reading

- Discuss the child's questions. Talk about how he or she might find answers to those questions.
- Prompt the child to think more. Ask: Preparing traditional foods is one way to honor one's heritage. In what other ways can we honor the past?

Pogo Books are published by Jump!
5357 Penn Avenue South
Minneapolis, MN 55419
www.jumplibrary.com

Library of Congress Cataloging-in-Publication Data

Names: Spanier, Kristine, author.
Title: Lithuania / by Kristine Spanier, MLIS.
Description: Minneapolis, MN: Jump!, Inc., [2023]
Series: All around the world | Includes index.
Audience: Ages 7-10
Identifiers: LCCN 2022024412 (print)
LCCN 2022024413 (ebook)
ISBN 9798885242035 (hardcover)
ISBN 9798885242042 (paperback)
ISBN 9798885242059 (ebook)
Subjects: LCSH: Lithuania—Juvenile literature.
Classification: LCC DK505.23 .S63 2022 (print)
LCC DK505.23 (ebook)
DDC 947.93—dc23/eng/20220524
LC record available at https://lccn.loc.gov/2022024412
LC ebook record available at https://lccn.loc.gov/2022024413

Editor: Jenna Gleisner
Designer: Molly Ballanger

Photo Credits: Ingus Kruklitis/Shutterstock, cover; Natallia Dzenisenka/iStock, 1; Pixfiction/Shutterstock, 3; asta.sabonyte/Shutterstock, 4; Nikolay Tsuguliev/iStock, 5; ljphoto7/iStock, 6-7tl; Alec Taylor/Shutterstock, 6-7tr; VladSokolovsky/iStock, 6-7bl; Kit Korzun/Shutterstock, 6-7br; ewg3D/iStock, 8-9; meunierd/Shutterstock, 9; STF/AFP/Getty, 10; Mindaugas Kulbis/AP Images, 11; PETRAS MALUKAS/AFP/Getty, 12-13; Oleg Nikishin/Getty Images, 14-15; Jonathan Ferrey/Getty, 16; Veja/Shutterstock, 17; LimeandLemon/Shutterstock, 18-19; Angel Villalba/Getty, 20-21; RomanR/Shutterstock, 23.

Printed in the United States of America at Corporate Graphics in North Mankato, Minnesota.

TABLE OF CONTENTS

CHAPTER 1

CASTLES AND CREATURES

Welcome to Lithuania! Would you like to visit a castle on an island? Trakai Island Castle is on Lake Galve. It was built more than 500 years ago!

Trakai Island Castle

Lithuania is in northeastern Europe. The Baltic Sea borders the west. The Curonian **Spit** stretches into the sea.

Curonian Spit

This country has around 3,000 lakes. About one-third of the land is forest. Lakes and forests make good homes for animals. Beavers and otters play in the water. Elk and wolves roam the forests.

WHAT DO YOU THINK?

The white stork is Lithuania's national bird. Does your country have a national bird or animal? Do you know what it is?

beaver

otter

elk

wolf

Vilnius

The largest city here is Vilnius. It is also the **capital**. The Neris River flows through it. Old Town is part of Vilnius. This area is more than 700 years old. Gediminas Castle Tower stands here. It is a **symbol** of the country.

DID YOU KNOW?

The Lithuanian flag flies at the top of Gediminas Castle Tower. Its colors have meaning to people here. Yellow is for **prosperity**. Green is for hope. Red is for courage.

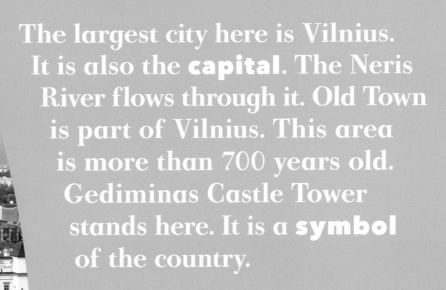

Gediminas Castle Tower

CHAPTER 2

FIGHT FOR CONTROL

In 1940, the **Soviet Union** took control of Lithuania. Lithuanians wanted their own government. They **protested**. In March 1990, they declared **independence**. Soviet troops attacked on January 13, 1991. Fourteen people were killed. The Soviet Union broke apart that year. Lithuania was free.

protest

Every year, Lithuanians remember those lost on January 13. It is called Freedom Defenders Day. People light candles for those who died. They place flowers at a **memorial**.

People here can vote when they turn 18. They **elect** members of **parliament**. It is called the Seimas. This group makes laws.

People elect the president, too. He or she works with leaders of other countries. The president also chooses the prime minister. This person leads the government.

ballot

presidential
flag

Lithuanian
flag

EU flag

The president lives in the Presidential Palace. Flags fly there. One is the Lithuanian flag. One is the **North Atlantic Treaty Organization (NATO)** flag. The **European Union (EU)** flag flies here, too. Soldiers raise the flags each morning. The flags are lowered each evening. People gather to watch.

NATO flag

WHAT DO YOU THINK?

Lithuania joined NATO and the EU in 2004. Leaders in these groups work to protect the freedom of countries. Do you think it is important to respect these flags? Why or why not?

CHAPTER 3

LIFE IN LITHUANIA

Basketball is the most popular sport in Lithuania. Many towns and cities have basketball clubs. Kids begin playing when they are young.

Children begin school the year they turn seven. In fifth grade, they begin learning another language. Most choose English. They can also learn German, Russian, French, or Latin.

Christmas is an important holiday. On Christmas Eve, families enjoy 12 **traditional** dishes. Most of the dishes are made from fruits, vegetables, and grains. Meat is part of the meal on Christmas Day.

TAKE A LOOK!

What are some of the most common Christmas Eve dishes in Lithuania? Take a look!

kūčiukai pastries

beet soup

herring

boiled or baked potatoes

sauerkraut

mushroom-filled crepes

Christmas bread

oatmeal pudding

cranberry pudding

nuts

dried fruit

poppyseed milk

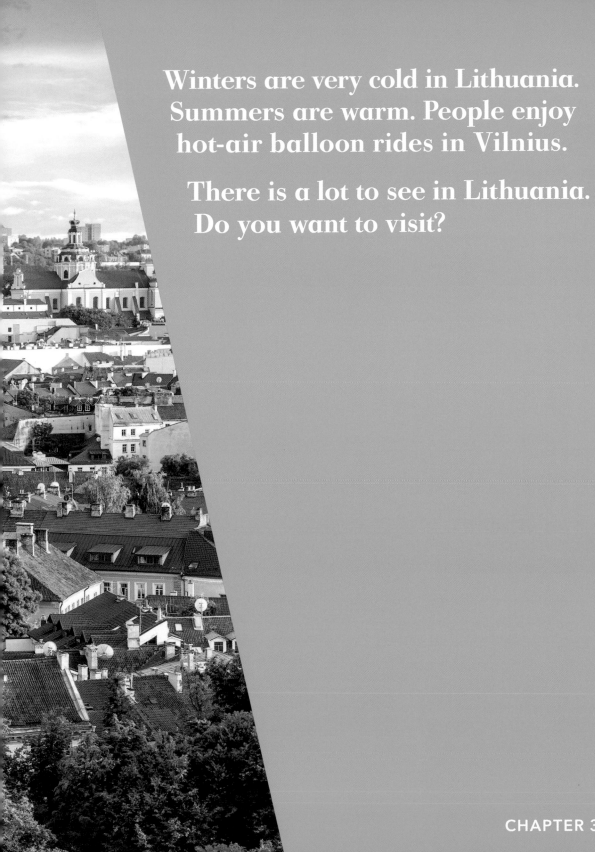

Winters are very cold in Lithuania. Summers are warm. People enjoy hot-air balloon rides in Vilnius.

There is a lot to see in Lithuania. Do you want to visit?

QUICK FACTS & TOOLS

AT A GLANCE

LITHUANIA

Location: northeastern Europe

Size: 25,213 square miles
(65,300 square kilometers)

Population: 2,683,546
(2022 estimate)

Capital: Vilnius

Type of Government:
semi-presidential republic

Languages: Lithuanian (official),
Russian, Polish

Exports: petroleum, furniture,
wheat

Currency: euro

capital: A city where government leaders meet.

elect: To choose someone by voting for him or her.

European Union (EU): A group of European countries that have joined together to encourage economic and political cooperation.

independence: Freedom from a controlling party.

memorial: Something that is built or done to help people remember a person or event.

North Atlantic Treaty Organization (NATO): An organization of countries that have agreed to give each other military help. This group includes the United States, Canada, and some countries in Europe.

parliament: A group of people elected to make laws.

prosperity: The condition of succeeding or thriving.

protested: Demonstrated against something.

Soviet Union: A former country of 15 republics that included Russia, Ukraine, and other nations of eastern Europe and northern Asia.

spit: A narrow strip of land that sticks out into water.

symbol: An object or design that stands for, suggests, or represents something else.

traditional: Having to do with the customs, beliefs, or activities that are handed down from one generation to the next.

Lithuania's currency

INDEX

TO LEARN MORE

Finding more information is as easy as 1, 2, 3.

1 Go to www.factsurfer.com

2 Enter "Lithuania" into the search box.

3 Choose your book to see a list of websites.

FACT SURFER